HORRIBLE HISTORIES®

HORRIBLE HISTORIES®

Terry Deary

Illustrated by Martin Brown

TERRIBLE TRAITORS

THE ORIGINAL AND THE WORST

SCHOLASTIC

Published in the UK by Scholastic, 2025
Scholastic, Bosworth Avenue, Warwick, CV34 6UQ
Scholastic Ireland, 89E Lagan Road, Dublin Industrial Estate, Glasnevin, Dublin, D11 HP5F

ISBN 978 0702 34481 7

A CIP catalogue record for this book is available from the British Library.

Printed in the UK.
Paper made from wood grown in sustainable forests and other controlled sources.

FSC www.fsc.org MIX Paper | Supporting responsible forestry FSC® C018072

10 9 8 7 6 5 4 3 2 1

www.scholastic.co.uk

For safety or quality concerns:
UK: www.scholastic.co.uk/productinformation
EU: www.scholastic.ie/productinformation

HERE ARE 52 PEOPLE WHO
HAVE BEEN CALLED TRAITORS ...
BUT ARE THEY ALL BAD?

YOU DECIDE.

TERRIBLE TRAITORS

CONTENTS

INTRODUCTION

Once upon a Tudor time there were three school children, Tom, Dick and Harriet. The three called themselves the 'Fantastic Four'. (They were not very good at maths.)

Just for a laugh, they sawed through the legs of their teacher's chair. When he sat down it fell apart and dumped him on the floor. He bruised his bum. The class of 52 children tried not to laugh. The teacher, Mr Thrasher, was furious. 'Which evil child did this?' he roared. Nobody spoke.

'Right,' Mr Thrasher said, 'If you don't confess, I shall beat every single child in the class till they bleed.' He took out his leather strap and waved it madly. Fifty-two children shivered in terror.

Then Dick – one of the Fantastic Four – stood up and said, 'Please, sir, it was Tom that held the chair while Harriet used the saw. They did it. I saw the saw.'

Tom and Harriet were punished horribly. Dick had betrayed them, and they called him nasty names.

And the worst word of all:

TRAITOR.

Tom, Dick and Harriet is just a story. But true history has always had someone who has switched sides or let down the people who thought they were a friend. Are YOU a traitor hater? Here are 52 people who have been called traitors … but they are not ALL bad.

AWFUL ANCIENTS

ENKIDU

(c. 2700–2500 BC)

The story of King Gilgamesh is said to be the oldest story in the world. It took place almost 5,000 years ago in the country we now call Iraq. It is a story of a man called Enkidu who rose up against the wicked king, Euechorsos. Rising against a king is 'treason' so Enkidu was a traitor. The world's oldest story is about a traitor.

One story says that the old gods declared that a baby called Gilgamesh would grow up to kill the king. What could the king do? What would YOU do? Yes, he snatched the baby from its nurse and threw it out of the window of a high tower. But you can't cheat the gods. An eagle swooped down and caught the baby Gilgamesh before he hit the ground and looked like a splodge of jam. The eagle landed in the palace garden to munch on a tasty tot.

But, what did I say? You can't cheat the gods?

The gardener came out with his spade and battered the bird and saved the child. Gilgamesh was returned to his mum, but she knew Euechorsos would try to kill him again. She put him in a basket and let it float down the river to safety.

Of course, when he grew up, Gilgamesh went back to Uruk and killed the evil Euechorsos – just as the gods had said he would. And the gods are never wrong. That's why they're gods.

Oh, how the people cheered … but not for long. If Euechorsos was cruel, then Gilgamesh was twice as bad. The people suffered (and stopped cheering). Something had to be done. What the Uruk people needed was a hero to stand up to Gilgamesh and a very hairy man called Enkidu was the man for the job.

The two men fought with swords all day and all night till at last Enkidu gave Gilgamesh a deep cut. The traitor Enkidu rushed forward to finish off his enemy, but he slipped on the blood of Gilgamesh and fell to the ground. Now it was the cruel king's chance to kill his enemy. But Enkidu cried, 'Stop. I have a message for you from the goddess

Ishtar. She wants you to go to Cedar Mountain to cut down a great holy cedar tree. Use it to build a new gate for the Temple of Enil in Uruk.'

Gilgamesh said, 'No one can cut down that tree. It is guarded by a monster.'

'Ah, but if you had me to help you we can defeat the monster together and do as the goddess wishes. What do you say?'

Gilgamesh said, 'Yes,' and that's what they did.

DID YOU KNOW?

Great gods and murdering monsters are just a tale. But some history writers think Gilgamesh was not just a fairy tale. They say that there really was a king, Gilgamesh. He was cruel to his people until one man, Enkidu, stood up to the bully king. They became friends and Gilgamesh learned to be a kinder man.

TARPEIA

(c. 800 BC)

Sometime after 750 BC the new city of Rome was in trouble. It served them right. They had attacked the Sabine tribe and pinched their women because they didn't have enough of their own.

Spurius Tarpeius was the Roman Army general who kept the Sabine army out. He had a daughter called Tarpeia. This young woman crept out of Rome and went to the Sabine camp.

'I say, you Sabine chaps,' she said. 'I can open a gate in the walls of Rome and let you in.'

'Sounds good, but why would you do that?' they asked.

'I want what is on your left arms.' Tarpeia was looking at their golden bracelets. If they gave her those, she'd be rich.

But they also carried their shields on their arms. They thought she meant their shields. So they threw their heavy shields at her and crushed her to death. Oooops.

Her body was returned to Rome and her corpse was thrown off the highest cliff in the city to be splattered on the sharp rocks below. After that, ALL traitors were thrown alive off that cliff and they named it the Tarpeian rock after the greedy woman.

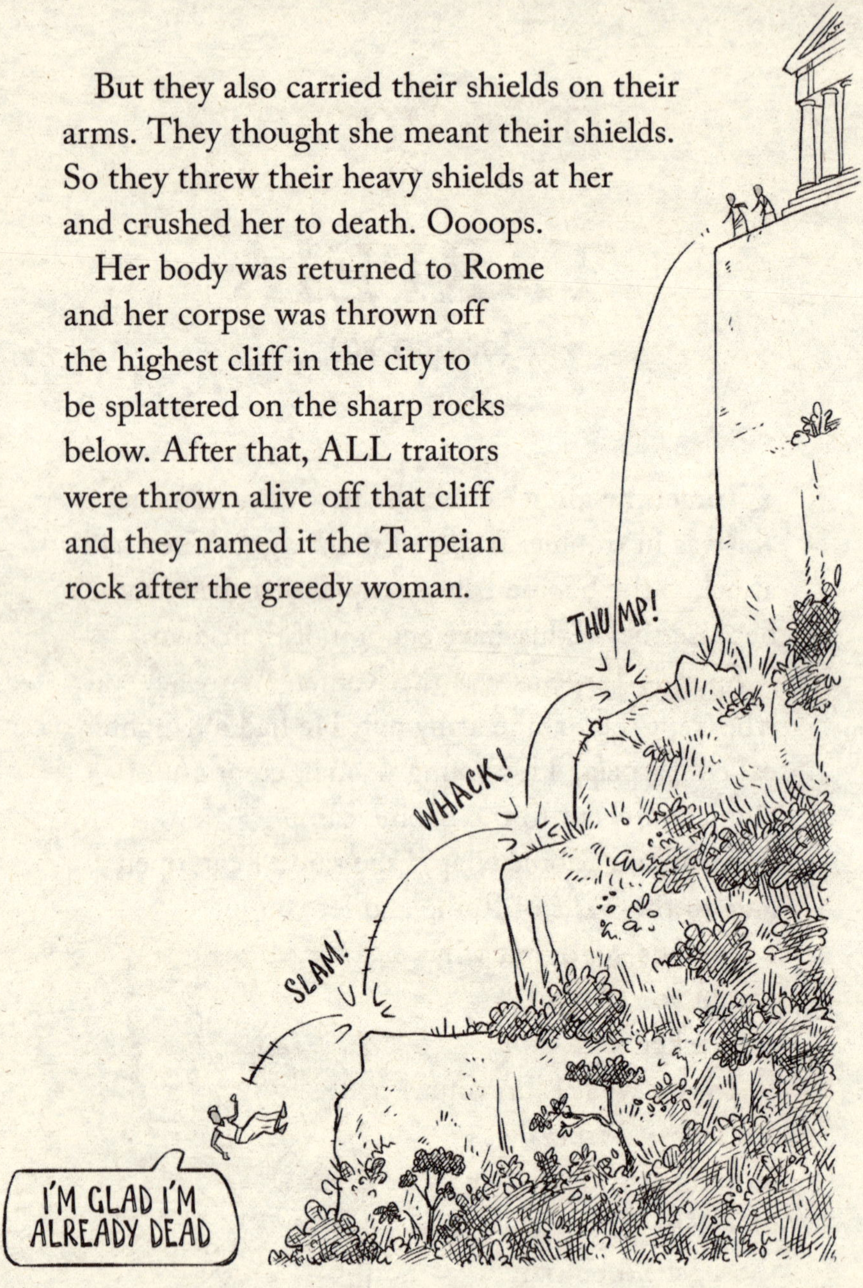

DID YOU KNOW?

Not everybody thinks Tarpeia was a traitor. She may have said...

That's the story they tell. But the truth is I wanted to help my dad and the Roman Army. I wanted the Sabine shields so they couldn't block the swords and arrows of my people. I would keep my promise and open the gate – but our army would be waiting to massacre them. Instead my death was sealed by iron shields of how I squealed.

A picture of Tarpeia being crushed by shields was stamped on some Roman coins so the Roman people would get the message: NEVER BETRAY ROME.

AWESOME EGYPTIANS

AY

(c. 1323–1319 BC)

Go up to a teacher and ask them, 'Can you name a king of Egypt?' Most of them will say Tutankhamun. (Some of them may say, 'Push off and stop annoying me you nasty little child.')

Tut is famous because his tomb was discovered in 1922 and was full of his riches. They have been seen by millions of people all around the world. He is famous. Dead famous.

Clever people still can't tell HOW he became so very dead. One idea is that he was murdered, and they blame his Uncle Ay. In 1968 an X-ray was taken of Tut's skull. It showed it had been cracked, maybe by a blow to the head. (A bit like you would be if you were hit by a two-ton-car … man.)

Tut was only 18 or 19 at the time. Awwww. But why Ay? Because

Ay married Tut's widow and took the throne. Sometimes a traitor may kill a king and WIN. Was Ay the guy to make Tut die?

Science is a lot better now than it was in 1968. A new scan seems to show Tut's skull was broken AFTER he died. It could have been the clumsy clowns who wrapped up Tut's body. Or Howard Carter – the man who uncovered the mummy in 1922. Now push off and stop annoying me you nasty little child.

DID YOU KNOW?

People who have tested Tut's mummy say there are other ways Tut may have died. Not a bonk on the conk.

MALARIA: The body shows the young king had quite a few attacks of malaria disease. The last one killed him.

INFECTED LEG: Tut's leg is broken. Did he have an accident? Did he fall off his chariot? Did he get germs in a wound that killed him?

POISON: Maybe Ay DIDN'T give his nephew a smack on the back of the head. But he DID get the throne and the widow. So, did he poison Tut?

MOHAMMED ABD EL-RASUL
(the 1880s)

In the 1800s the people in Europe started to uncover the graves and mummies of ancient Egypt. The people of Egypt found there was a lot of money to be made from it. They would rob the graves and ship them off to museums in Europe and America. They were grave-robbers.

In 1880 a French archaeologist called Gaston Maspero set out to stop them.

Three Egyptian brothers called el-Rasul had found 30 mummies near their village of Qurna, and it was like a treasure chest to them. They dug them up and sold them.

Gaston Maspero arrived and arrested the brothers. They swore, 'We are not grave robbers,' and all the villagers agreed the family were honest.

Gaston called in the local police, who tortured the brothers. Not one of them betrayed the others. But the oldest brother, Mohammed el-Rasul, was furious. He suffered a lot and said, 'I deserve HALF of all the money we make.'

The rest of the family refused. So, Mohammed betrayed them to the police. He showed them where they found the mummies. He said that one day, 20 years before, a goat belonging to brother Ahmed had strayed and Ahmed followed the bleating of his animal. It had fallen down a deep hole. Ahmed climbed down after it and found himself in a poky corridor, cluttered with dark shapes. He lit a candle and saw that the shapes were a collection of dusty wooden coffins heaped one upon another.

They sold the treasures for 20 years till Mohammed betrayed them. The mummies were sent to a museum in Cairo, Egypt. The dead kings and queens must have liked that.

And what happened to traitor-brother Mohammed? Mohammed was paid the huge sum of £500 (worth almost £77,000 today) for being a traitor. His family must have hated that.

DID YOU KNOW?

Mohammed may have betrayed his family, but he saved the mummies from being sent all over the world. They stayed in Egypt where they belonged.

Gaston Maspero had to return to France, but he needed someone in Egypt to guard the graves. Who was the best man to do that? Traitor Mohammed Abd el-Rasul of course. He had the reward AND a good job. Sometimes it pays to be a traitor.

GROOVY GREEKS

SINON

(c. 1183 BC)

The story of the Wooden Horse of Troy is one of the oldest stories in the world. We don't know if it is true or a legend. It is probably a bit of both.

The Greek armies set off to attack Troy but couldn't break down the walls. So they sat there for ten years … some say from 1193 till 1183 BC. That could be true.

The Greeks decided to build a huge wooden horse and pack it with soldiers. They then packed their tents and pretended to go away. The Trojans said, 'Ooooh, look. The Greeks have left us a prezzie. Let's bring it inside so everyone can see it. It'll be a main attraction.'

They pulled the wooden horse into their city – at night the soldiers climbed out and opened the gates.

How could the Trojans be so STUPID? One story says a Trojan called Sinon was a Greek spy. He stayed behind when the Greeks pretended to sail away. He told the leader of Troy, Prince Paris, 'The Greeks built it as a gift to the goddess Athena (who likes horses). Take it inside and Troy will be blessed.'

Pin-brained Paris fell for the trick. Sinon opened the secret door in the Wooden Horse and let the Greeks out to murder the people of Troy and capture the city.

DID YOU KNOW?

People are digging at the ruins of Troy to find the truth. They have found that old Troy WAS destroyed – walls tumbled, houses burned and skeletons of the dead have been uncovered. Was it an earthquake? Or a Greek attack from the outside? Or a wooden horse from the inside? We may never know.

PAUSANIAS THE REGENT

(born c. 510 BC, died between 470 and 465 BC)

Pausanias the Regent was a Spartan general in the wars against Persia. But he was a traitor. One day the Spartan leaders told him to return to Sparta to go on trial. The order must have looked like this:

General Pausanias,

You are ordered to return to Sparta at once and stand trial. It is said that you...

1 ...have given Spartan secrets to Xerxes I, king of Persia. In return he said you could marry his daughter.

2 . . .have released Persian Prisoners. After your army captured Byzantium, you set enemy prisoners free because they were relatives and friends of the Persian king, Xerxes.

3 . . .have started acting like a Persian and dressing in Persian clothes.

4 . . .plan to make yourself master of Greece.

5 . . .want to help our Spartan slaves revolt against their masters.

Pausanias was guilty and would have been executed, but he ran off to a temple where the executioners could not spill his blood. So they didn't. They blocked up all the temple doors and left Pausanias inside to starve to death.

DID YOU KNOW?

Everybody in Sparta was sure Pausanias was a traitor – even his own mother. When they started to lay bricks to shut him in, his mother asked if she could lay the first brick.

The Spartan life was brutal and you had to be tough to survive. If a baby looked weak when it was born it was left on a hillside to die – or be eaten by wild animals.

ROTTEN ROMANS

BRUTUS

(85–42 BC)

When Rome was built they had kings. But they were awful people, so the Romans said 'No more kings. We will have the wisest and richest men to rule us. Put them together and call them a "senate". But not the women. Sorry, ladies.'

And so it went on for 500 years. Then Julius Caesar came along and was a great warrior. 'I am so great I could lead the whole country. A bit like a king really.'

A lot of those wise and rich senators hated the idea. Others didn't mind. After all Caesar was winning the world for Rome and making them richer.

But, in the end, the Caesar-haters won. Caesar came to the senate. He thought he was there to sign some papers. Instead the enemy senators pulled out daggers and stabbed him 23 times. Now, if you're a leader then your enemies are dangerous, but your friends can be far more deadly. Brutus was the man Caesar trusted and he came up with the last stab. Some say Caesar was so sad to see Brutus attack him with a knife he couldn't bear to look – he pulled up his toga and covered his eyes. He might have said something like, 'Oh, no. Not you as well, Brutus.'

DID YOU KNOW?

The Romans split into two sides – the friends of Brutus and the friends of Mark Antony. Mark Antony won the last great battle. When Brutus saw he had lost, he killed himself. His head was cut off and sent back to Rome where it was thrown on the senate floor – it landed near the statue of Caesar. His body was burned. When his wife learned that Brutus was dead, she killed herself too. The families of traitors can suffer as well.

ARMINIUS
(HERMANN THE GERMAN)
(18 BC–AD 22)

In the year AD 9 Emperor Augustus put his nephew Varus in charge of the armies in Germany.

One German chief, Arminius (also known as Hermann), pretended he was a friend. He went to Varus and said, 'There is a rebellion in the north. Send your armies. Take a short-cut through Teutoburger Forest.'

A massive thunderstorm lashed the Romans as Arminius led them deep into the forest. Arminius had 20,000 men hidden in the dense woodland.

The paths twisted and forked, climbed over rocky ridges and dropped into boggy swamps. When they reached the deepest, darkest part of the forest, Arminius dashed off and abandoned Varus. The paths were muddy and the Roman wagons were bogged down.

The Romans got stuck. The German rebels struck. The Romans were slaughtered. Women, children and camp followers were all killed. There were tales of Romans being sacrificed to the German gods. They were cooked in pots and their bones used for ceremonies. Some captured Romans were placed inside wicker cages and burned alive.

Six years later the Romans sent a new army to north Germany. When they reached the forest they found heaps of white Roman bones and skulls nailed to trees. Their guts had been strung out over the tree branches.

That sounds horrible. But remember the Romans could be even more horrible. They took prisoners from the places they conquered and sent thousands to be executed in the arenas. Thousands cheered as poor men and women died. The Romans had to be stopped. And Arminius stopped them at the River Rhine. After this battle the Roman Empire never spread north, and the Germans stayed free of Roman rule. Hermann the

German became a German hero ever after.

DID YOU KNOW?

A Roman legion had between 4,000 and 6,000 men. Varus had three legions in Germany, the 17th, 18th and 19th legions. Along with their families and servants there would have been around 20,000 men, women and children who went into the Teutoburger Forest. The Romans never again used the numbers 17th, 18th and 19th for their legions – they were unlucky.

Varus fell on his sword and killed himself.

SPIES

MITHRIDATES THE GREAT

(132–63 BC)

Mithridates was king of Pontus (northeast Turkey) when he was a teenager. But the lords thought he was too young to rule. They put his mother, Laodice, in charge. She wanted his brother to take the throne. Mithridates had to die.

Assassins had poisoned his father and now they set out to kill Mithridates. He had to flee and disguised himself as a beggar to escape. Mithridates would have to become a rebel and a traitor to win back the throne from his mother.

He did it in a very cunning way. He had learned 22 languages by the age of 14 – always useful for a spy – and wandered through Turkish cities and learned about their defences. He was one of the world's first spies. After a few years he knew all about the weaknesses of the cities and the best ways to capture them.

He returned and his small army easily took over the cities one by one. In the end he had enough power to grab his throne.

Mithridates's mother and brother had been ruling the country – he had them executed. He became a hero of the Pontus people and defeated the Romans many times. Eventually he lost a battle and he ordered a servant to kill him with his sword.

DID YOU KNOW?

Some poisons kill a human because their bodies are not used to it. Mithridates was worried about being poisoned like his dad. So, he took little drops of poison every day. If anyone tried to put poison in his food it wouldn't work. In the end, he tried to kill himself with poison to avoid being captured by the Romans, but because of his daily drops it didn't work, so he had to use a sword instead.

CHRISTOPHER MARLOWE

(1564–93)

Christopher was known as 'Kit' Marlowe. He could have been as great as William Shakespeare if he had lived. The trouble was, he seemed to enjoy spying as much as writing.

Elizabeth I was hated by the Catholics in England. There were 200 plots to kill her. She needed a spymaster to hunt for the plotters and she gave the job to Sir Francis Walsingham. Kit was one of his spies.

Some people thought Kit was a Catholic. They started to think that the only reason he spied on Elizabeth's enemies was so he could betray Walsingham and warn the assassins. Kit was called to a meeting with three of Walsingham's most deadly spies, Marlowe was stabbed in the eye and died. The spies said they had a quarrel about who should pay the bill for their dinner.

Was that true? Or was Kit 'executed' because his spymasters thought he was a traitor?

DID YOU KNOW?

Kit Marlowe's greatest play was about a character called Doctor Faustus. He met the Devil and made a deal: Doctor Faustus would have all the power in the world but only for 24 years. After that time the Devil would return and take the Doctor's soul to burn in Hell for the rest of time.

Doctor Faustus found that great power was no fun after all. Selling his soul was a big mistake.

CUT-THROAT CELTS

ANDROGEUS

(c. 54 BC)

Cassivellaunus, a Celt leader, fought against Julius Caesar when the Roman landed on the south coast of Britain in 54 BC. With the help of another Celt leader, Androgeus, Cassivellaunus drove the Romans back for a while. There was a party to celebrate and for fun there was wrestling. In the fight, one of Cassivellaunus's family was killed by one of Androgeus's family.

Cassivellaunus wanted the killer handed over to be punished. Androgeus refused. Cassivellaunus said, 'Hand him over or I will attack you.'

Androgeus didn't think he would win a war with Cassivellaunus. He needed help. Who did he go to? Yes, he ran to Caesar and said, 'Help me.' What a traitor.

When Caesar returned, Cassivellaunus led an army against him again. As Cassivellaunus faced the Roman enemy, Androgeus attacked Cassivellaunus from the rear with 5,000 men. Cassivellaunus lost the battle and had to make peace with Caesar.

DID YOU KNOW?

The Romans advanced to London and lined up on the south bank of the Thames. Cassivellaunus and his Britons stood with swords and spears on the north bank. The Britons waited, daring the Romans to cross. Their fierce faces were painted blue with a plant that grew along the Thames – woad.

Then, from the south came a monster. A war elephant. With its huge help, Caesar defeated the Britons. Then he went home to Rome before winter storms left him stranded in Britain.

CARTIMANDUA

(ruled c. AD 43–69)

After Caesar, the Romans invaded Britain again in AD 43 and the Celts tried to fight back. Their greatest leader was Caratacus. If he'd been able to write he might have told this story.

I did NOT run away. When the Romans attacked I 'retreated' to fight another day. That's not running away, is it? I went to Wales in the summer of AD 48 and stirred up the Silures tribe there. I became one of the first ever Welsh heroes, I did.

We attacked Roman convoys to Wales … and we attacked the tribes that had surrendered. People like the Dobunni. We put them to the fire and the sword. We sort of murdered other Celts. But those rotten Romans still beat you in the end. I didn't run away, of course. But I did retreat. Again.

I gathered my men for one last great battle. We had a steep slope behind us and a river in front of us. There was no way the Romans could defeat us. I told my friends it was freedom forever or slavery. Oh, how they cheered me. They knew we couldn't lose.

But we er . . . lost. The Romans actually crossed the river. Captured my wife, the kids, my brothers. Disaster. Of course I ran – I mean retreated. I ran as far as the Pennines and went to Queen Cartimandua of the Brigante tribe. I knew she'd help me. I didn't know she'd made a deal with the Romans, did I? She promised to do what they told her.

She was a lovely lady. She said, 'Why not come into my private room and put your feet up. It's a long walk from Wales.' And I said, 'Sounds like a good idea to me.' We had a party. And as soon as I was full of wine and had fallen asleep, she fastened me in chains and handed me over to the Romans. I mean, what sort of traitor does that? Cartimandua.

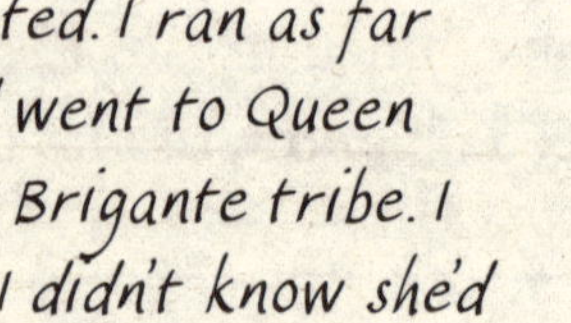

You'll be taken to Rome and put on display. Then in front of all the Roman people you'll be strangled to death. Not much of a party, Carti.

DID YOU KNOW?

Caratacus was led to Rome in chains. He expected to be executed. But when he got to Emperor Claudius he made the famous speech that saved my life. He said, 'I am a great warrior and killing me will not bring the Romans glory. But if you let me live I can show how great and powerful you are.' He went on to live a life of luxury in Rome.

SMASHING SAXONS

HENGIST

(born c. AD 420, died 488)

If a friend invited you to a party, would you say 'yes', then go to the party and stab them before they had even served the jelly and custard? That would be a trifle treacherous. But that's what the Saxon warrior Hengist did.

The Celt king Vortigern invited Hengist and his Saxon warriors to fight against the Scots to the north. A monk called Gildas told the story...

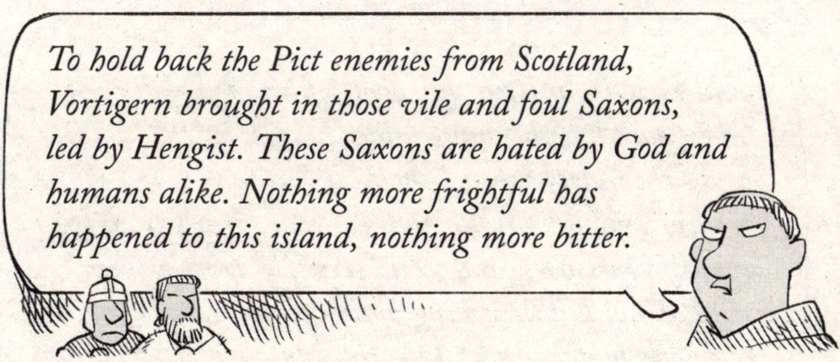

Then Vortigern made an even bigger mistake. He fell in love with Hengist's daughter, Rowena and Hengist gave her to Vortigern. Then Hengist said, 'Now give me half of your kingdom.'

Vortigern tried to fight back.

All the great towns fell to the Saxon battering rams. Bishops, priests and people were all chopped down together while swords flashed and flames crackled. It was horrible to see the stones of towers thrown down to mix with pieces of human bodies. Broken altars were covered with a purple crust of clotted blood. There was no burial except under ruins and bodies were eaten by the birds and beasts.

Then the two enemies agreed to make peace. The Saxons came to a feast with all the great warriors of Vortigern. What happened next is known as the night of the Long Knives. A monk wrote...

And Hengist ordered the whole of his men that each one should hide his knife under his foot in the middle of his shoe. And when I shall call out to you and say, 'Draw your swords,' then draw your knives from the soles of your shoes, and stand strongly against them. And do not kill their king but seize him for the sake of my daughter. And all the three hundred lords of King Vortigern were slaughtered.

Hengist was a ruthless man. He didn't mind using a sneaky trick to murder Vortigern's lords. And he didn't mind using his daughter to marry Vortigern so he could rule England: 'Do as I want, or I'll take your wife away.' How would you like it if your dad married you off to get what he wanted?

DID YOU KNOW?

Vortigern was not the leader's actual name. Vortigern is just an old word that means 'Great King'. Except he wasn't that great, was he?

EADRIC STREONA

(c. AD 975–1017)

The Viking King Cnut invaded Britain and Saxon King Edmund II stood in his way. A Saxon called Eadric Streona thought Cnut would like it if he assassinated Edmund and would give Eadric a rich reward. He didn't get what he expected. Picture him sitting under a huge tree and writing a letter…

Dear Mum,

Just a quick note to say goodbye. As you know, I killed King Edmund at a feast. I went to the toilet pit and lay down in the dark under the king's seat. When he

sat down I took out my long knife and stabbed him in the bum. He died very quickly, and I got very messy. I'll never get the poo out of my pants.

Anyway, I went to the Viking King Cnut and told him that I had got rid of his greatest enemy. 'Will you reward me?' I asked. 'I shall raise you higher than any English lord,' he promised. And here I am under the tallest tree in England. He is going to hang me from the highest branch. I'll be higher than any English lord, see? Very funny, Cnut.

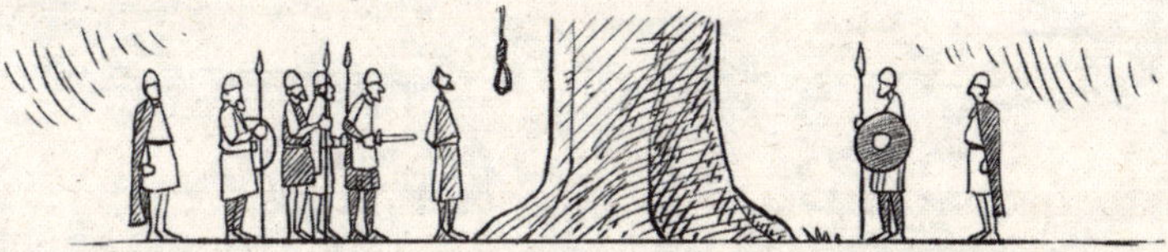

The Vikings plan to cut my head off and put it on a pole over London Bridge while my body will be thrown in the River Thames to rot.

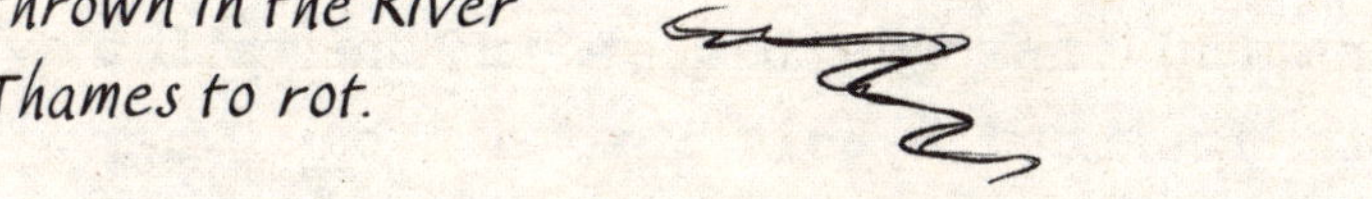

At least my head will be high up and I'll have a lovely view.

Here come the Vikings with their rope now. So it's bye bye, Mum. Nice knowing you.

Your loving son,

Eadric

Eadric was called 'Streona' because it means 'grasping' or 'greedy'. Eadric was a real rat. He changed sides from English to Dane when it suited him. At the battle of Ashingdon he was fighting for King Edmund II … yet chopped off an English soldier's head and held it in front of the English army. He cried out, 'Run for your lives. Our king Edmund is dead.' The real King Edmund ripped off his own helmet and called out, 'No, I'm not. Fight on'.

DID YOU KNOW?

The French writer Geoffrey Gaimar wrote that Edmund was killed with a booby-trapped crossbow hidden in the toilet pit. It fired a bolt into his bum when he sat down. The arrow went in so far they couldn't get it out. He was buried with the arrow. But there were no crossbows in England at that time. It was a lie.

IRELAND

GRACE O'MALLEY

(c. 1530–1603)

Grace O'Malley (1530–1603) was born into a family of Irish sailors and traders … though some called them pirates. They lived on the West Coast of Ireland and if you wanted to sail through their waters you had to pay – either cash or some of your cargo.

Grace wanted to be a sailor like the rest of her family. But her father told the young girl, 'Your long hair would tangle in the ropes.'

Grace was furious. She dressed like a boy and hacked her hair till it was short as a sailor's. Sorted. She told her father she was ready to sail with him. Her family laughed and gave her a new nickname: Grainne Mhaol (Grace the Bald). Her father gave in and they set sail for Spain. On the way they were attacked by an English ship. Her father told her to get safely below the decks. Instead she climbed up a mast. From her perch she spotted an enemy creeping up behind her father with a knife raised.

Grace dropped onto the man's back, kicking, biting and screaming. The terrified man fled and so did the rest of the English. She had saved her father's life. Their pirate ways made them outlaws.

In 1593 Grace's son was arrested as a rebel, so Grace went to London to ask Queen Elizabeth for his release. The two women were nearly the same age – about 60 when they met at Greenwich Palace.

Grace wore a fine gown but had a hidden dagger. Guards found it before she could attack the queen. To kill the queen wasn't simple murder – it was treason. Grace said she only had the dagger to protect herself. Queen Elizabeth believed her.

Grace refused to bow down to Elizabeth because she said Elizabeth wasn't the queen of Ireland.

Still, Elizabeth liked Grace O'Malley, and they reached an agreement – Elizabeth would sack her wicked Irish governor and Grace would stop her pirate ways. They each kept their promise but only for a while.

Both women died in the year 1603.

DID YOU KNOW?

A lot of Irish hated being ruled from England. They think Grace O'Malley is a hero. Elizabeth I's governor in Ireland was making the Irish suffer. Grace was just fighting back.

Grace married the vicious Donal O'Flaherty – it was said he murdered his nephew when he thought the boy was getting too much power. Nice man.

ROBERT EMMET

(1778–1803)

In 1798 the Irish rose up against their British rulers but were defeated. In 1803 the United Irishmen rose again. This time led by 24-year-old Robert Emmet. Only about 80 joined him – and they weren't very good traitors…

The United Irishmen were in a pub when the landlord arrived with some news. 'Your enemies, the British Army, know you are going to attack tonight. They will be waiting for you.'

The 'secret' attack wasn't secret anymore. Their attack was never going to work.

- They had explosives to blow down the walls of Dublin Castle. A week before the attack the explosives went off by accident.

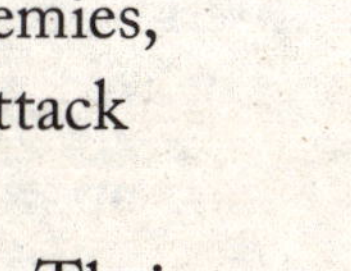

- The United Irishmen armed themselves with grenades – but no one could find the fuses to set them off.

- There was a traitor in the group of traitors. He sent a message to the United Irishmen to say 'it's off'. Many of the Irish believed him and went home.

- Without explosives to blow the walls down, they decided to climb over them. Just before they attacked, they found there was only one ladder.

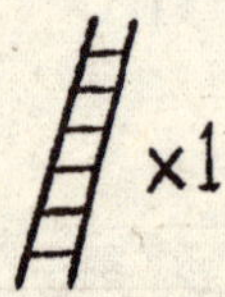

- They planned to ride to the castle. But a rebel set off a pistol. That scared the horses, so they bolted and left the rebels to walk.

- The rebels panicked as they got near the castle. 'British soldiers are told that soldiers are approaching.' They rushed forward but found it was just a crowd of people coming out of the pubs at closing time.

- Leader Robert Emmet called off the rebellion before it had really started and went into hiding.

Robert Emmet was caught and taken to the scaffold to be hanged before he was cut up. He climbed a ladder and had the rope placed round his neck. It was the executioner's job to take the ladder away.

The executioner asked, 'Are you ready, sir?'

Emmet said, 'Not yet.' This went on a few times. Emmet kept saying, 'Not yet.'

The hangman was so fed up with waiting he took the ladder away anyway. Emmet died saying, 'Not y…'

DID YOU KNOW?

After Emmet was hanged, he was cut into quarters. His followers tried to dip handkerchiefs in the martyr's blood as a souvenir ... but dogs beat them to it and lapped it all up.

VICIOUS VIKINGS

THE VIKING WIFE

(around the AD 800s)

In history many men think a wife should do everything they are told. If they don't, the wife is a traitor. But some men deserve to be betrayed. A Viking wife may have put this in her diary when her vicious Viking husband gave her an odd order…

My husband Gunnar is always getting into trouble in Bergthorshvall and I was fed up with him. He was a bully and a troublemaker. He picked fights. But he made a B-I-G mistake. Once – just once – he slapped my face. I couldn't fight back – he was too strong – but I knew I'd get my revenge one day. Today was the day.

He upset our lord and was told to get out of Iceland or

die. He chose to stay and fight. This morning the lord's warriors arrived to arrest him. Gunnar refused to leave the house so they surrounded it. 'I'll kill every last one with my arrows,' he laughed. (He did a lot of that.) He began firing and the warriors fell until ... disaster. His bowstring snapped. He cursed. (He did a lot of that too.) He looked at me and stroked my hair. 'Lovely hair,' he said.

'Thanks,' I said. 'You don't usually say nice things about me.'

'Lovely long hair,' he said. 'Long enough to make me a new bowstring.' He pulled out his knife to cut it off. 'Can I take it?' he asked.

All I said was, 'Remember the day you slapped my face?'

'Yes,' he said.

'Then NO,' I said.

'I'll not ask you twice, you traitor,' he said proudly. He opened the door and went out to fight to the death with his sword. He died bravely, like a Viking should. Such a shame. But he'll not be slapping my face again.

DID YOU KNOW?

Some Vikings used women as slaves. You may think those enslaved women would be pleased to see their enslaver die? No, because a dead warrior was put in a boat that was set on fire to cremate him. The enslaved woman was expected to die in the flaming boat.

ALFRED THE GREAT

(c. AD 847 to 849–899)

When the Vikings invaded England they landed in the north and east and drove the English back to the south and west. The Vikings occupied a part of England that was later called Danelaw.

One leader who tried to fight back was King Alfred the Great. His kingdom was Wessex. But to beat the Viking invaders from Denmark he had to become a traitor.

He pretended to be a minstrel and walked into the Danish camp to sing for them – and spy on their battle plans.

The next day, Alfred went back to his Saxon army. He knew the Danish battle plan and was able to beat it.

This story was first written down five hundred years after Alfred's death, so we can't check if it's true. But it goes to show, even a singer can be a traitor.

STORMIN' NORMANS

WALTER TIREL

(c. 1065–1100)

William the Conqueror's oldest son was called William. How boring is that? He grew up to be greedy and bad tempered. He had red hair and an even redder face, so he was given the nickname Rufus … that's Latin for 'red'.

A monk wrote…

> *He was very harsh and fierce in his rule over his country and towards his people and to all his neighbours. He was always annoying his nation with robbing and unfair taxes. Everything that was hateful to God was the daily habit in this land during his reign, so he was hated by almost all his people.*

The big bad bully Billy decided to go hunting deer one day. His arrow-maker brought him six new arrows. He picked the best four and gave two to the knight Walter Tirel. 'That's fair, isn't it? The sharpest arrows should go to the sharpest shot.'

Just before he left a letter arrived from the abbot of Gloucester. It warned the king that there was danger if he left the safety of the castle. William ignored the warning and set off into the New Forest and waited quietly by a deer track for an animal to come along. Walter Tirel stood at the other side of the track.

A deer trotted down the path. Sharp-shot Tirel fired but missed. Oh, deer. The arrow flew across the path and hit the king in the chest, killing him on the spot. (It could have been worse … Tirel could have hit the poor little deer.)

No one is sure if it was an accident – that was Tirel's story – or murder. But think about it…

- If Tirel was such a good shot, how could he miss something as big as a deer completely?

- Or was he a brilliant shot who hit the little target he was aiming at … the king's heart.

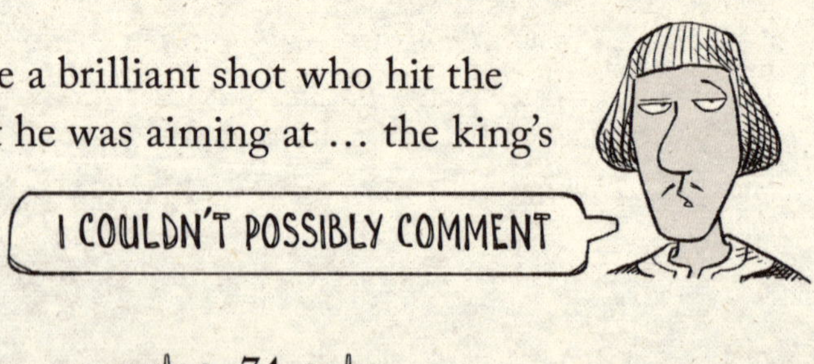

The deer must have thought, 'Gosh, that was an arrow escape.'

DID YOU KNOW?

William died while hunting in the New Forest on 2 August 1100. The crown went to his enemy, and brother, Henry I. But, did you know, that on 2 August 1100 Henry just happened to be out hunting ... in the New Forest? Was he part of a plot to kill Will?

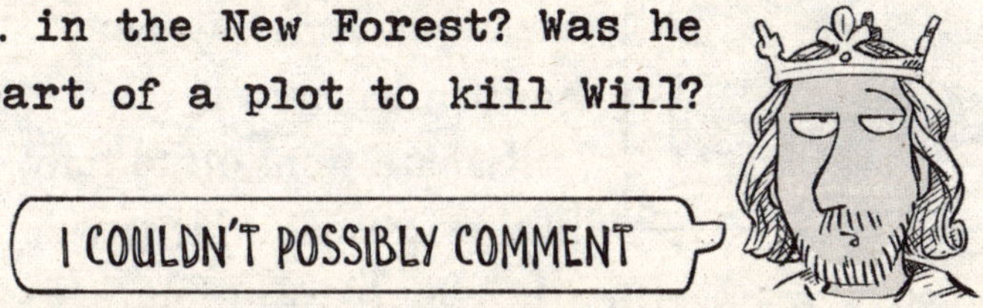

The king's body was placed on a cart and taken to the cathedral at Winchester ... blood dripped from the body all the way. He was buried in the tower there. The next year, the tower fell down.

KING JOHN
(1166–1216)

'Treason' is betraying your king or queen. But sometimes kings have been traitors. Sometimes lords snatched the throne from a king. But John tried to grab the crown from his own brother, Richard I.

Richard went off to fight in the Crusades. He left ministers to look after the country. But John set up his own government. He then went on to tell everyone that Richard had died and said he should be king.

Richard was alive and came back to England. He forgave John after a while. Then Richard died – horribly with a crossbow bolt in his neck that poisoned him – when he went to fight the French.

Richard said his nephew Arthur should be given the English crown. John had other ideas. His army captured Arthur in a siege and took him to a castle in Falaise, France for a feast but made him a prisoner. A monk wrote…

> **King John had captured Arthur and kept him alive in prison for some time. At length, in the castle of Falaise, after dinner on the Thursday before Easter, when John was drunk and possessed by the devil, he killed Arthur with his own hand, and tying a heavy stone to the body, threw it into the River Seine. It was discovered by a fisherman in his net, and being dragged to the bank and recognised, was taken for secret burial, in fear of the tyrant.**

John was hated by almost everybody and is said to be the worst king England ever had. It's reported that he died from eating peaches. They gave him bad stomach pains and a fever that killed him. A thunderstorm raged on the night of his death. That was God being angry, the people thought. His bad bowels were buried at Croxton Abbey, while his body was taken to Worcester Cathedral for burial.

DID YOU KNOW?

John upset the Pope and the Catholic priests. They accused him of being a devil. A werewolf, in fact. After his death, his body was heard to be moving in its grave ... it couldn't rest under holy earth. So a group of monks dug him up and buried him outside the graveyard.

ENGLAND

EMPRESS MATILDA

(1102–1167)

In 1135 King Henry I was dying. (Awwww, what a shame.) He had just one child, Matilda and she would take Daddy's throne. (Ahhhh, that's nice.)

But … (uh-oh). Her cousin Stephen said HE should be king of England. (What cheek.)

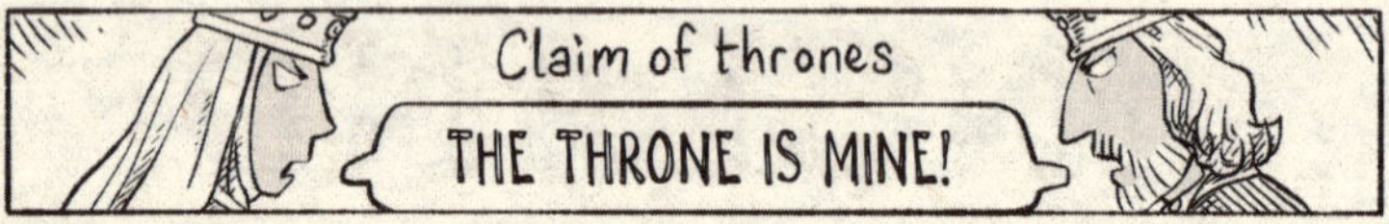

Even worse for Matilda … most of the great lords of England agreed with Stephen. (Why?)

- England had never been ruled by a queen – she can't lead England's armies into war.

- Matilda was a bit bossy and wouldn't listen to the barons' advice.

* The barons DO like Stephen and so do the people of London.

* She married Geoffrey of Anjou and the people of Anjou are always at war with the people of Normandy.

Stephen was crowned. And Matilda said, 'This means war.' But who was the traitor? Matilda fighting against the king? Or Stephen for fighting against the queen? Who knows?

Their armies battled in England for 19 miserable years.

* Villages were burned, crops were ruined or stolen.

* The land was lawless so the lords could kidnap and torture the rich until they paid for their freedom.

* Food was hard to find or very expensive to buy, so people starved.

* Soldiers raided towns to burn homes and steal from the helpless families.

For *19* years. (Wow.)

Matilda captured Stephen when he lost the Battle of Lincoln in 1141 but she had to let him go – Stephen's friends had captured her brother and said they'd kill him.

Then Matilda herself was captured at Devizes. She escaped by pretending to be dead and was carried out as a corpse. In 1142 she was held in Oxford Castle, but again she managed to escape. A story says it was in a snowstorm while the guards were sheltering indoors. Matilda was lowered from the castle walls on a rope. No one saw her escaping across the snowy fields. Why not? Because she wore a white cloak. (That's clever.)

Matilda escaping in the snow

DID YOU KNOW?

In the end they made peace. Stephen stayed king and when he died Matilda's son took the throne. (Sorted.)

QUEEN ISABELLA

(1295–1358)

Princess Isabella was the daughter of Philip IV of France. She became Queen Isabella of England … but her most famous name was 'She-wolf of France'. And it wasn't because she wanted to eat Red-Riding-Hood's granny. It was because she was so ruthless.

She married Edward II of England in 1308, but in the 1320s he had a favourite family who became advisers to him. The Despensers. Isabella hated them. Oh, how she howled.

Isabella sailed for France in 1325 where she was later joined by her son (the young man who would become Edward III). She refused to return to England until the Despensers were thrown out of the royal court.

To help her, she became friends with Roger Mortimer and, with other barons who hated the Despensers, they crossed to England in 1326. In the battle that followed they smashed the forces of Edward and the Despensers.

The head of the hated family, Hugh Despenser the Elder, was beheaded. Hugh Despenser the Younger suffered the full traitor's death of hanging, drawing and quartering.

Was the She-wolf upset as she watched her enemy's guts spill out? No, she was not. As he died, she enjoyed an apple.

Not everyone in England liked her. Many barons rose up against her. When the nobles rose against her, what did Isabella do?

a) Run back to France 

b) Send her son Edward to fight the rebels 

c) Put on armour and go to fight them herself 

Answer: c) She dressed in armour and rode a war horse to meet them. They surrendered and hoped she would spare them. She didn't. She had them all executed as traitors.

DID YOU KNOW?

Her husband Edward II disappeared, and most people believed he was murdered at Berkeley Castle. Some reports claim he was killed by having a hot poker shoved up his bum and burned from the inside. Others said he was smothered in his sleep. Either way he was dead as a chicken in a nugget.

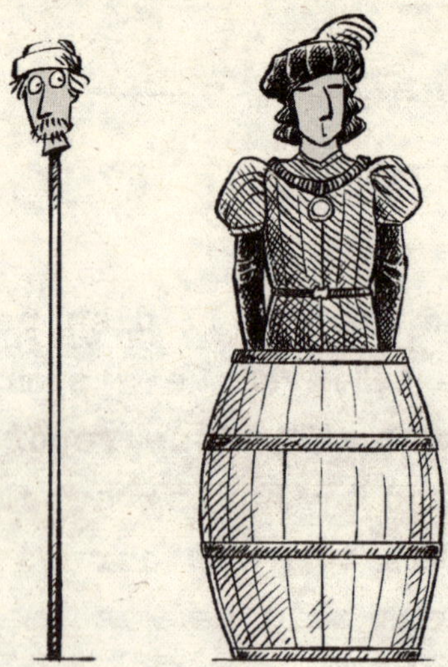

MEASLY MIDDLE AGES

WAT TYLER

(c. 1341–1381)

In 1381 the peasants of England were poor and hungry and worked to death by their lords. Then a new 'Poll' tax caused more trouble. It's a tax on every 'head' or 'poll' – and as most people had heads, most people had to pay it. The peasants were led by Wat Tyler, and his ragged army marched through London to see the king. They lopped off a few lordly heads along the way and stuck them on poles. (They probably fastened them on with pole tacks.)

Wat Tyler finally got to meet the king on the banks of the River Thames. After a failed negotiation, the king declared Tyler a traitor to the angry crowd. One of the king's men said, 'Tyler, you're the greatest thief and robber in the whole of Kent.'

Wat was furious. He drew his dagger and rode towards the king. Mayor Walworth of London drew his own dagger and stabbed Wat. The king's squire, Ralph Standish, joined in and ran his sword through the rebel a few times.

Somehow Wat staggered back to his horse and his friends took him to a house to care for him. The king's men dragged him out and chopped off his head. He may already have been dead by then, of course.

Wat Tyler had been murdered. No one else wanted his risky job. The peasants gave up and went home. End of the Peasants' Revolt.

DID YOU KNOW?

The peasants went home after Wat was killed. But the lords were scared and things DID get better in time.

DUKE OF CLARENCE

(1449–1478)

Duke Richard was a ruthless man. His brother was King Edward IV. They had another brother – George and he was lots of trouble. George became Duke of Clarence. While their big brother King Edward was still alive, George was a real nuisance. He acted like a spoiled child.

- In wars against Edward IV, Clarence supported the enemy side led by the Duke of Warwick. He even married Warwick's daughter to make them like blood brothers.

- He tried to say Edward IV was not the son of their father – so George should be the true king.

- When Edward IV's wife died, George said Edward IV had poisoned her. He then tried to stop Edward IV marrying a second wife, Elizabeth.

- When his wife Isabel died, he tried to blame Edward IV for having her poisoned.

- He plotted to have Edward thrown off the throne. He sent his son over to France to raise an army to rebel against Edward.

Edward IV had to get rid of George and the traitor was sentenced to death. A story says that the duke had his head stuck in a barrel of wine until he drowned.

Another story says it was Richard III (before he became king) who carried out the execution.

DID YOU KNOW?

George said Edward had cheated so he could get his bum on the throne. How did Edward cheat? George said he used witchcraft ... witch is totally batty.

CASTLES

ROBERT II OF NORMANDY

(born around 1051 or 1054, died 1134)

William the Conqueror conquered Normandy, conquered England, conquered Wales and then he stopped. He must have run out of conkers.

William the Conqueror had squabbling sons. Robert II of Normandy (1051–1134) argued with his younger brother, King Henry I (1068–1135), who had become king of England. Robert tried to invade England to take his brother's crown. He failed and was thrown into prison from 1106 until 1134. He spent his last few years in Cardiff. Then he died. But he had always been trouble. He had even fought against his own father, William, and nearly killed him. William the Conqueror might have written a terrible toilet story in his diary…

My Robert has always been lazy and weak. Greedy too. I made him Duke of Normandy. I visited him there.

Two of my other sons – William and Henry – played a wicked joke on him. William and Henry played dice with Robert. They grew bored. They left the gaming table and crept onto the balcony above. They filled a toilet pot full of pee (and other stinking matter). They then tipped it over Robert's head. Robert didn't think it was funny.

He flew into such a rage he attacked his brothers. I had to come between them. Robert cried like a baby and told me that I should punish them. I didn't.

His revenge was foul as that toilet pot. He tried to attack my castle at Rouen.

Robert attacked his own father who was his ruler in Normandy. He attacked his brother, the ruler of England. He had the heart of a traitor. THAT is the sort of person Robert was, so you may not feel too sorry for him locked away in Cardiff Castle. But if you hear one tale you probably WILL feel sorry.

Horrible Histories warning: this story is REALLY horrible, told by a monk...

He died in Cardiff aged over 80.

IFOR BACH

(c. 1150–1211)

In 1158 Cardiff Castle was the scene for a daring kidnapping carried out by one Ifor Bach (Ifor the Short). Ifor Bach said he was a Welsh lord in the south of Wales. The Normans arrived and took over. Ifor wanted his land back.

The Norman castle in Cardiff looked too strong to attack … still Ifor decided to climb the castle walls one moonless night. The guards didn't see him. He found himself in the bedroom of the Earl of Gloucester's wife, Lady Gloucester.

There were no newspapers at that time, as you know, but if there HAD been, they may have looked like this...

THE CARDIFF REPORTER

IFOR CROSS WITH LADY GLOSS

Reports are coming in of a daring raid on Cardiff Castle by its old owner Ifor Bach. After climbing the walls, he found Hawise Lady Gloucester in her bedroom. Servants report hearing her scream, 'Who's there? William. William. There's someone in the room. Let me light a candle - where's the tinder box...'

Ifor Bach replied, 'Don't scream, Lady Gloss or I may have to cut your throat. And you are more use to me alive.' He went on, 'This is MY land, and your husband stole it from me.'

The French wife of Lord Gloucester cried, 'Stole? No. He is the rightful lord - the king conqueror said so.'

'I don't care what King Kong says. He can't monkey with me.' It seems Ifor didn't understand everything she said. Ifor turned nasty.

He threatened to cut her son's throat if her husband didn't sign over the land to him. 'I would kill him very slowly - and probably let you watch. Then I'd kill your husband even more slowly. And finally, I'd kill you so very slowly you'll beg me for death. How does that sound my lady?'

'A bit messy to be honest,' she replied.

Ifor said he was taking her with him, and she would be held hostage until Bach got his land back.

What will happen next? Read tomorrow's *Cardiff Reporter* to find out.

What do you think happened next?

a) The Duke of Gloucester agreed to give the land back.

b) The Duke of Gloucester refused to give the land back, so Ifor killed Hawise and Robert.

c) The Duke of Gloucester refused to give the land back, so Ifor married Hawise.

Answer: a) Reports say the Duke of Gloucester agreed to giving back Bach's land. So, hijack Bach wins.

SCOTLAND

WILLIAM WALLACE

(c. 1270 – 1305)

William Wallace is a hero in Scotland. He is remembered as 'Braveheart'.

The punishment for fighting against the king or queen of England was to be punished in a truly horrible way. The traitor was hanged till he was half dead then let down onto the ground. He was cut open and his guts pulled out and burned on a fire. He was then beheaded and his body cut into quarters. These quarters would be sent to the biggest cities in the country and lifted up on a pole for everyone to see and say, 'This is what happens to traitors.'

One of the first men to die this way was William Wallace in 1305. The English King Edward I ruled Scotland. The Scots wanted freedom and they rebelled. Their leader was Wallace. After years of fighting Wallace was captured and taken to London for trial.

He said, 'How can I be a traitor to Edward when Edward has never been my king?'

His execution was meant to crush the Scots and make them agree to have English Edward as their king. It didn't work. William Wallace was seen as a martyr who died for Scottish freedom. They fought even harder.

DID YOU KNOW?

Wallace's story was told in a film in 1995 called 'Braveheart'. But it didn't tell the true story.

- **Wallace was shown as a fighter who painted his face like an ancient Briton – he didn't.**

* He was shown as a common man but the real Wallace was a noble and would have called himself 'Sir' William Wallace.

* The next great Scottish leader was Robert the Bruce. He was known as 'Braveheart', not Wallace.

So don't believe all the stories you read in books and films – unless it's a *Horrible Histories* book of course.

JAMES 'WEAVER' WILSON

(1760–1820)

The last person sentenced to being hanged, drawn and quartered was a Scottish weaver called James Wilson. The weavers in the 1820s were weaving flax. The price of flax went up and nobody wanted the weavers' cloth anymore. The weaving families starved. They went on strike. But they were told that they were traitors. Their leaders, like James Wilson, had to be punished.

THE FLYING SCOT

1 September 1820

WEAVER WILSON PAYS PRICE

James Wilson, the sixty-year old rebel leader, was brutally executed yesterday. The weavers' leader was fastened to a wooden sledge and dragged to a scaffold in front of the law courts in Glasgow. The old man wore an open-fronted shirt over his white prison uniform and white gloves. His mysterious travelling partner wore a black mask and carried an axe.

Last week Wilson was found guilty of treason. In April he had marched from the village of Strathaven at the head of a small group of rebels. Wilson was armed with a rusty old sword and his followers had poor weapons. When they arrived in Glasgow they found the city was quiet and there was no support. They were easily arrested and brought to trial.

The judge sentenced Weaver Wilson to suffer the ancient form of execution like William Wallace, to be hanged, drawn and quartered. A crowd of 20,000 gathered to watch the gruesome spectacle and there was a large guard of Dragoon soldiers to prevent trouble.

Wilson was hanged and died bravely. He was then cut down and beheaded with a single stroke of the axe. The executioner held up the white-haired head and cried, 'Behold the head of a traitor,' as was the old custom. The crowd jeered and hissed in disgust, crying, 'shame' and 'murder'.

Some of the soldiers fainted at the sight. It was decided to spare Wilson's corpse the disgrace of being cut into quarters. He was thrown into a pauper's grave in Glasgow, but his niece had the body dug up and returned to the churchyard in his Strathaven home.

Wilson's supporters have been distributing leaflets telling his true sad story and saying, 'May the ghost of the murdered Wilson haunt the pillow of his cruel judge.'

Next week the rebels Baird and Hardy will go to a similar death in Stirling. Isn't it time Scotland gave up this barbaric punishment? No man deserves to die the way Wilson died. The judge called him a 'miserable and sinful creature.' Many poor Scots will see him as a martyr for a free Scotland.

DID YOU KNOW?

New weaving machines took more jobs and the weavers had even less. In 1837 they went on strike again. No one was hanged but the leaders were sent to Australia as prisoners for seven years.

A hundred years after Weaver Wilson

died, the poor workers were STILL living horribly. In 1905 a report said 'A man, his wife, his son, two daughters, and his wife's mother share a single room 3 metres by 4 metres. There are six toilets for the 429 people in this tenement block.'

TERRIFYING TUDORS

ALICE ARDEN

(c. 1516–1551)

A traitor in Tudor England was someone who tried to harm their lord. When a woman married a man, HE became her lord. Harming your husband was treason and you would be executed horribly.

Henry VIII closed the monasteries and sold the lands. Thomas Arden of Kent bought a lot of those lands and became rich. But his wife fell in love with a man called Richard Moseby and wanted Thomas Arden dead.

She tried to poison him but failed. Thomas Arden ate a couple of spoonfuls but said it tasted unpleasant. He lived.

What she needed was a team. She got John Green to help; he was a tailor who hated Thomas. One of her servants agreed to help and then she added George Bradshaw, a goldsmith and ex-soldier. Finally, they added a killer, Will of

Calais who charged Alice £10 to join the gang.

Will had a couple of goes at murdering Thomas. He planned to attack the man as he rode home alone from London, but Thomas met up with a group of friends and Will had to wait for another chance. Will added his friend George Shakebag to the team and planned to kill Thomas on a ferryboat. But sat-nav hadn't been invented and Will got lost.

At last Will and Shakebag managed to kill Thomas in his home on Valentine's Day 1551. They dragged the body through a snowstorm and dumped it in a field. But then it stopped snowing. Rotten luck. The local law men were able to follow the footprints of the killers back to Arden's house where they caught the killers red-handed.

At the trial Alice was found guilty of treason. Her punishment wasn't hanging – instead she was burned alive.

DID YOU KNOW?

The story of Alice Arden was remembered for a hundred years, thanks to a play that was written called 'Arden of Faversham'. Some teachers think the famous poet and playwright William Shakespeare may have done some of the writing.

MARGARET CLITHEROE

(c. 1556–1586)

Henry VIII got rid of the monasteries because they were Catholic, and he wanted to force people to join his own church – the Church of England. His daughter Elizabeth took the throne and also tried to ban Catholics. It was against the law to be a Catholic priest or even give one shelter. One woman died horribly for doing just that…

- In 1571 Margaret (aged 15) married butcher John Clitheroe of the Shambles in York and they had three children. John, her husband, was a Protestant but had a brother who went to train as a Catholic priest in Reims, France. A death sentence for the butcher's brother if he were caught.

- Margaret Clitheroe in York City was Catholic

and let priests have Catholic services in her home. She risked a horrible death for being a traitor to Queen Elizabeth.

- Someone told the law officers that she had hidden a Catholic priest and she was arrested. Who betrayed Margaret? Her own son.

- She was taken to court and asked to plead guilty or not guilty. But there was a catch. If she pleaded 'guilty' she would be executed, but her children would be left with no one to care for them. If she pleaded 'not guilty' her children and servants would be tortured till they betrayed her.

- She refused to plead. The law had a special punishment for that. It said:

Criminals who stand mute are to be pressed to death by huge weights laid upon a board that lies on their chest, and a sharp stone under their backs.

* Margaret shrugged and said, 'God be thanked, I am not worthy of so good a death as this.'

* Margaret was taken to the bridge over the River Ouse in York so a large number of York people could watch and learn a lesson.

* No one wanted the job of pressing the woman to death. At last seven beggars agreed to take on the grim task.

* The woman was stretched out on the ground with a sharp rock under her back and a door was placed over her. Stones were placed on top of the door. Despite the increasing pain she still refused to say guilty or not guilty.

* Eventually her bones were broken, and she died within 15 minutes.

DID YOU KNOW?

You can go to The Shambles in York today and see Margaret's house. The Catholic Church made her Saint Margaret Clitheroe.

WALES

BLACKSMITH MADOG

(around the 1280s)

In 1282, Llywelyn, Prince of Gwynedd, raised the Welsh in revolt against King Edward of England.

Llywelyn burned Edward's castles and fought Edward's troops. Edward was furious and wanted him executed as a traitor. But while Llywelyn was away gathering a new army, the English attacked first.

The Welsh were beaten near Builth Wells. They say 3,000 Welsh surrendered, and put down their weapons – then the English slaughtered them.

Llywelyn heard the battle and rushed back. But it was a trap. He'd been betrayed.

The story says that when Llywelyn got to Orewin Bridge he met an English knight, Stephen de Frankton, who challenged him to a fight.

Llywelyn was the most wanted man in Britain – but this Stephen de Frankton had no idea he was fighting the Prince of Wales.

Llywelyn wasn't wearing any armour – just a tunic. Stephen de Frankton charged at him with a lance and ran it through him. Then when he found out who he'd killed, he cut off Llywelyn's head and put it on show in English towns.

We're not sure if Llywelyn turned up without armour at the bridge because of a traitor. A story says the prince had been hiding in a cave to keep out of English hands. One morning he rode up to the blacksmith called Madog at Aberedw with a clever plan. He said, 'I want you to take the shoes on my horse and put them on backwards.' When English trackers followed his trail they'd be confused.

The blacksmith did that, but later turned traitor and told the English where to find the prince. Madog got the nickname Min Mawr … Big Mouth.

DID YOU KNOW?

It wasn't just Big Mouth who was blamed for being a traitor. The people in the nearby town were blamed too. For years the poor people of Builth were called bradwyr Aberedw. Aberedw traitors.

OWAIN GLYNDWR

(c. 1354–1415)

Owain Glyndwr was a traitor to the English. He is a hero to the Welsh because he fought for Welsh freedom.

Owain Glyndwr was one of the richest Welsh landowners. BUT his revolt in 1400 wasn't about the posh people like Owain. It was a revolt of the peasants. Some of the Welsh peasants working in England even went home to take part.

Owain gathered 270 rebels and attacked and burned Lord Grey's estates at Ruthin.

The English tried to crush the revolt, but storms smashed the English army. The rebels said God was on their side and they made Owain their Prince of Wales. English King Henry had already said his son was Prince of Wales, so he was a bit annoyed. He said Owain was a traitor and had to be destroyed.

Owain Glyndwr could be pretty cruel in war, even when he was winning.

- The castle keeper at Peterston surrendered. Owain had him beheaded anyway.

- Owain took Radnor Castle, 60 prisoners surrendered. They were all executed.

- Owain's men wrecked the towns they defeated. Even 120 years later they still felt the effects. In Tudor times Sir John Wyn wrote…

> *I visited the towns of Hay and Radnor, and they still bore the scars of Glyndwr's revolt. Green grass grew on the marketplace in Llanrwst, and the deer fed in the churchyard.*

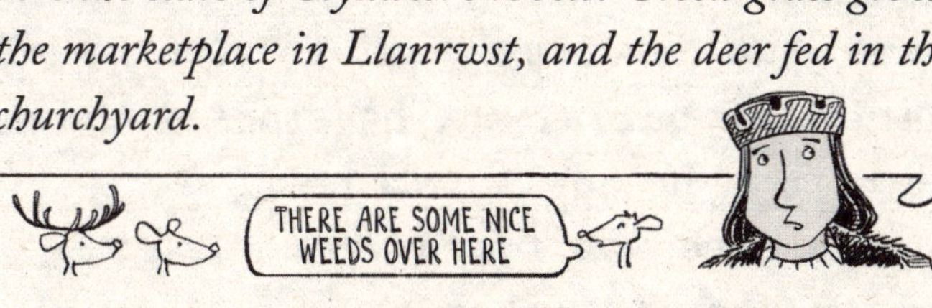

It was Henry IV's son – the 'other' Prince of Wales – who defeated the Welsh. In 1405 he butchered a Welsh army at a battle near Usk and the war turned against Owain Glyndwr. Owain's son was hacked to death and 300 Welsh soldiers were beheaded by the River Usk.

No one is sure what happened to Owain. He disappeared. He may have died at his sister's house in 1415.

But the poor never forgot him. In the 1700s Thomas Pennant collected the stories of Owain that made him out as the chief hero of the Welsh. They say he's still alive. Sitting in a cave playing chess with King Arthur, waiting for the day when the Welsh need a hero to save them.

DID YOU KNOW?

Owain was a pretty ruthless man. Even his own family could suffer if they crossed him. Owain killed his cousin Hywel. Then he burned his house to the ground. But he didn't want to give Hywel a Christian burial. So, he stuffed the corpse in a hollow in an oak tree. A rotted corpse was found years later – just cinders and ashes.

ROTTEN RULERS

RICHARD III

(1452–1485)

When Edward IV died, the crown of England was supposed to go to his son – Prince Edward. But Edward IV's brother, Uncle Richard, snatched the boy and locked him in the Tower of London. Prince Edward was never seen again, and Richard took the crown to become King Richard III. Most people think he had the little prince murdered.

As Prince Edward was the rightful king, Richard III was a traitor.

William Shakespeare wrote a play about Richard III and made Richard look as if he…

* Murdered Prince Edward and his little brother, Prince Richard.

- Had a twisted body as well as a twisted mind.

- Killed his brother Clarence as well as the little princes but also said he killed his own wife, Anne.

- Murdered Anne's father and husband so he could marry her himself.

He even wrote that Richard lost his final battle against Henry Tudor because he was exhausted. Guilty nightmares had haunted him all night.

DID YOU KNOW?

Richard III got rid of young Prince Edward and became king, but only lasted for a couple of years. Along came Henry Tudor who fought Richard at the Battle of Bosworth. He became Henry VII, the first of the Terrible Tudors.

Henry Tudor beat Richard the thirder,
When the battle turned into pure murder,
He pinched Richard's crown for the ride back to town,
He was top man ... he could go no furder.

OLIVER CROMWELL

(1599–1658)

If rebelling against your king makes you a traitor, then Oliver Cromwell was the most traitorly traitor to ever tread the trails of England. He led the army of Parliament that fought King Charles I, captured him and had him beheaded.

In life Oliver's head was described as ugly. He had a huge wart over his right eye and a big red nose – he was given nasty nicknames like 'Copper-nose', 'Ruby-nose' and even 'Nose Almighty'.

In 1658 he died – if he hadn't he'd be over 400 years old by now. His ugly head was treated as badly as Charles I's.

* 3 September 1658. Oliver dies aged 59. Doctor Bates examines the body. He says the brain weighs 6 ½ pounds. He prepares the body for pickling. A French book of the 17th century describes how to do this:

The brains should be put into a vessel with the bowels and the blood.

* The empty head is packed with lint cloth and sewn up. The body is wrapped in a green cloth like an Egyptian mummy.

* May 1659. Parliament invites Charles II to become king. Doctor Bates is suspected of having poisoned Oliver … and becomes a hero.

* 4 December 1660. Parliament votes to dig up Oliver, drag the body to the scaffold for hanging.

* 30 January 1661. Twelve years since Charles I was executed, Oliver's body is hanged from 9 am till 6 pm at Tyburn gallows, London. At sunset the body is cut down and beheaded. Because he'd been pickled and wrapped, it takes eight chops with the axe to remove the head. The head is stuck on a 6-metre pole.

* Charles II's revenge for his dad's beheading is done.

DID YOU KNOW?

On 25 March 1960 the head was given to Oliver's old college, Sidney Sussex in Cambridge where it is buried. A sign in the chapel says he is buried nearby ... but not the exact spot. They don't want it to be stolen by people who hated him for killing a king. It's still there today.

Even a successful revolutionary leader can face a terrible revenge once the revolution is over.

SLIMY STUARTS

GUY FAWKES

(1570–1606)

Guy Fawkes is famous for the 1605 Gunpowder Plot to blow up King James when he went to open Parliament. Barrels of gunpowder were stacked up in the cellars below Parliament. Guy was given the job of lighting the fuse to set them off. That would make him a traitor. But was there a bigger traitor? Was there a man who betrayed the plotters?

Guy was caught at least twelve hours before Parliament was due to meet the king. And it wasn't 'luck'. Someone in the plot had written to Lord Monteagle, a member of the House of Lords, to warn him: 'Stay away from the opening'. Monteagle passed on the message to the king and James was saved.

But what traitor wrote that letter? Most people believe it was one of the plotters, Francis Tresham. Lord Monteagle was married to Tresham's sister and Tresham didn't want her to see her husband blown apart.

Guy was tortured on the rack for two days before he even gave his real name. It took another two days before he confessed to the plot, then six more days before he named any other plotters. But, by that time, his partners had already been hunted and arrested or killed. They had been betrayed … but not by Guy Fawkes.

One of the plotters arrested was Francis Tresham. He was taken to the Tower of London but fell ill and died there.

DID YOU KNOW?

Guy was due to be hanged, drawn and quartered. He'd be hanged slowly so he would suffer while being cut open. When he reached the scaffold he stepped up the ladders for the hanging but he jumped so he died quickly and cleanly.

TITUS OATES

(1649–1705)

Titus Oates (nitwit)

Why did the Brits hate the Catholics? Because they believed they were plotting a Catholic take-over of the country. Why did they believe that? Because a man called Titus Oates said so.

Why did the Brits believe Oates? Because they were STUPID.

Oates was known as 'Filthy Mouth'. So-called because his nose ran all the time and the snot dribbled into his mouth. He liked to get very drunk. He was accused of stealing neighbours' pigs and chickens.

King Charles II was walking in St James's Park

in August 1678 when a friend brought a message from Oates and Tonge…

> *There are two Catholic gunmen waiting in the park to shoot you. As soon as you are dead the Catholic King Louis XIV of France will invade Britain.*

Charles II was as clever as you and he said, 'Rubbish.' But the king's council met Tonge and Oates who swore the story was true.

Then one of the magistrates who was investigating the case went missing. Five days later his battered body was found on Primrose Hill in London. He had been stabbed with his own sword after he'd been beaten to death. Gruesome and sinister. The Catholics got the blame, of course.

Panic spread and dozens of people were arrested and executed. The king's doctor was found guilty and hanged till he was half dead, revived so he could see himself being cut open and his intestines burned on a fire. In all, 35 innocent people died horrible deaths because of Oates's lies.

After two more years of this terror, Charles II died. His Catholic brother, James II came to the throne, and it was time for revenge. Titus was taken to the pillory where he was pelted with eggs and rubbish for two days. On the third day he was stripped to the waist, tied to the back of a cart and made to walk behind it while he was whipped.

This was repeated the next day when he was dragged on a sledge while he was whipped because he was too weak to walk. He spent three more years in prison before being released when James II fled from England. James's Protestant daughter, Mary, took his throne.

DID YOU KNOW?

Mary was happy her dad was dead and she became queen. She bounced up and down on the palace beds.

USA

BENEDICT ARNOLD

(1740–1801)

Ask an American to give you the name of a traitor and most of them will say 'Benedict Arnold'.

In 1776 the British settlers in North America rebelled against King George III and his government back in Britain. They began a Civil War against the British leaders. When they won the war they called it 'The American War of Independence'.

Benedict Arnold was a Brit living in America and he fought for the settlers. He helped to capture the Fort at Ticonderoga, then he was wounded in the leg at the battle of Saratoga. He thought he should get a higher rank in the army. He didn't. He was cross.

Benedict was short of money and George III's army offered him £20,000 to join them.

He gave American secrets to the British enemy but when his army discovered his treason he fled. He then fought for his new Brit friends.

DID YOU KNOW?

Rebel leader Thomas Jefferson was desperate to get his hands on Bad Benedict to get some revenge. He heard Arnold had been wounded in the leg. The same leg he'd been wounded in fighting for the rebels. He said...

They never did catch him, and Bad Ben moved to England. He was never very popular with anyone, not even the Brits, and still had no money when he died.

GEORGE WASHINGTON

(1732–1799)

When the British in America decided to rebel against King George III they formed an army. Every army needs a general and the top rebel was George Washington. He had fought for the British against the French and the Indigenous Americans, so he knew what he was doing.

He was trusted by the rebels because he was said to be honest. The most famous story is about Washington and the cherry tree.

George Washington and the Cherry Tree

Once upon a time there was a boy called George. When George was six, his father gave him a present – a little axe. As you know it is a daft thing to give boys axes. Young George went around the garden chopping things. He ended up chopping down his dad's favourite cherry tree.

Oh, Dad was upset. 'Who's been chopping my tree?' he roared. 'They deserve a smack on the ear.' Young George bravely said, 'I cannot tell a lie, Dad; you know I cannot tell a lie. I did cut it with my little axe.'

His dad's anger vanished. He gave George a hug and said, 'Truth is worth more than a thousand trees.'

And let's hope he took the axe off the little wrecker George.

The end

The rebels won the war and America got the freedom they wanted. Britain couldn't fight a war at a distance of 3,000 miles. The rebels created a new country, the United States of America, and chose a president instead of a king. They picked leading rebel fighter, George Washington, to be the first president.

DID YOU KNOW?

In 1748 a schoolboy copied out rules from a French book that told children how to behave. He wrote, 'Do not clean your teeth with your fork, your knife or the tablecloth.' Clean your teeth with a tablecloth? Sadly the boy who wrote that mustn't have cleaned his teeth with anything because he ended up with false teeth. People thought they were made of wood because they were so brown. The boy's name was George Washington and he grew up to be America's first president. By the time he became president he only had one tooth left in his head. The rest were made from elephant tusks, animal teeth or human teeth pulled from enslaved people.

BRITISH EMPIRE

TIPU SULTAN

(1751–1799)

The British invaded other lands and took over. They added them to the British Isles to make a British Empire. It was a cruel empire that made a fortune from enslaving Africans and robbing rich countries like India. The amount they took from India might be worth 63 TRILLION pounds today.

But the French had an empire too and they wanted to use the people of India to drive out the British. They trained Tipu Sultan from Mysuru (southern India) to raise an army and fight the British. The British saw him as a traitor.

The British raised an army of 60,000 soldiers from Britain and India. Tipu Sultan's had about half that number – around 30,000.

In 1799 he was safe in the fortress city of Srirangapatna. The British couldn't get to him … unless there were traitors inside the fort. And there were. They were Tipu Sultan's own ministers.

They were very sneaky and made the walls of the fort weak – the stronghold became a weakhold. The British forces were able to break through, enter the fortress and kill Tipu Sultan.

That's what traitors do best – pretend to serve their leaders but plot against them.

DID YOU KNOW?

Tipu famously said, 'Better to live one day as a tiger than a thousand years as a sheep.'

But a dead tiger is not so good as a sheep that lives a thousand years. Wouldn't ewe agree?

Quick Quiz

The Brits had two weapons to finally kill off Tipu … what were they? Pick two out of the five.

1 Catapults
2 Cannon
3 Elephants
4 Traitors
5 Treacle

Answer: 2 and 4. The cannon blasted a hole in the wall around Srirangapatna while Tipu's traitor general let the Brits rush in. Brave Tipu rushed to defend the hole in the wall. In spite of four deadly wounds, he fought on till he was finally shot down. Tipu's body was found after the battle – under a pile of other bleeding corpses.

GENERAL ANDRIES CRONJÉ

(1849–1923)

In the days of Queen Victoria the British Empire was growing larger and larger as Britain invaded more countries. The Dutch Empire had done the same, including in South Africa, where large numbers of Dutch-speakers (the Boers) settled. They objected to the British attempts to acquire the land they had taken, and this led to a great war where the Boers aimed to drive out the British armies.

South Africa was a foreign country to the British and they had no good maps. They needed Boers to show them around … Boer traitors. The Brits set up the National Scouts Corps and Boer traitors joined them to help their enemy, the Brits.

Even some top Boer soldiers joined the British. General Andries Cronjé had been a Boer leader at the start of the war. But after a defeat he surrendered to the enemy. Instead of being locked away in a prisoner-of-war camp he joined the British National Scouts to help fight against his own people. A real traitor.

DID YOU KNOW?

The National Scouts were called Hensoppers by the loyal Boers. Hensoppers means what?

1 Hen suppers because the Brits rewarded them with chicken dinners every day.

2 Hands-uppers because they put up their hands to surrender.

3 Hens hoppers because they hopped around like panicking chickens.

Answer: 2) If you wanted to insult someone in your Boer town you called them hensopper or National Scout. Those became swear words. What they really meant was 'traitor'.

GORGEOUS GEORGIANS

ARTHUR THISTLEWOOD

(1774–1820)

In 1820 Arthur Thistlewood had a plan as daring and deadly as Guy Fawkes: he would kill the Prime Minister and attack the chief ministers at dinner. Their heads would be cut off and stuck on poles. They would take control of the most important buildings in London and get the whole country to revolt.

The traitor Thistlewood DIDN'T know there was a traitor in his rebel gang – George Edwards – who would spill all their secrets to the police, known as the Bow Street Runners. George made sure Thistlewood and friends were walking into a trap.

The plotters met in a hayloft above a stable in Cato Street. The rebels fought back, and a Bow Street Runner was shot dead. Some plotters were arrested, Thistlewood and a couple of others escaped but were later captured. Eleven men were tried for treason. Five leaders were sentenced to death. They were hanged and had their heads cut off while crowds watched. One was set free and the other five sent to Australia.

Arthur Thistlewood and the Cato Street plotters were fighting against the government that was letting British people starve. The poor workers didn't have a vote so they couldn't change their miserable lives.

DID YOU KNOW?

The wives of the executed plotters asked if they could have their husbands' bodies – and the heads – so they could bury them in proper graves and lay flowers. But the prison said no. The bodies were buried inside Newgate Prison and covered in 'quicklime' so they dissolved.

Quick Quiz

Two of the traitors who were sent to Australia ended up with a strange job. They became what?

a) Gravediggers
b) Policemen
c) Hangmen

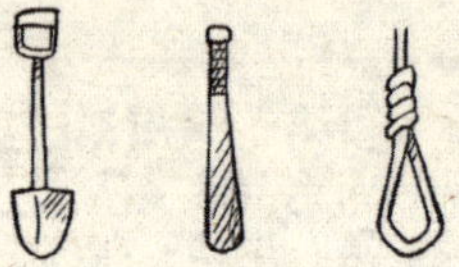

Answer: b) They ended up with better lives than they had back in England. It was worth being traitors … except for the famous five who lost their heads.

BONNIE PRINCE CHARLIE

(1720–1788)

King James II lost his throne in 1688 because he was a Catholic. He was from the Scottish Stuart family and his supporters – especially in Scotland – wanted the Stuarts back on the throne of Britain. They were known as Jacobites and they rebelled in 1715 and 1745, the later rebellion led by James' son Prince Charles – or Bonnie Prince Charlie.

When Charlie landed at Eriskay Island on 23 July 1745, he had only a magnificent seven supporters, yet he planned to conquer Britain. This number rapidly increased, and Charlie led 5,000 clansmen into England. Surprise, surprise, the English didn't want his dad, James, to be king. Charlie turned

around and marched back to Scotland. Even bigger surprise: a lot of the Lowland Scots didn't want a Stuart king again. The Bonnie Prince was upset.

He thought it couldn't get worse. At Culloden, near Loch Ness, he would face a monster defeat from the British Redcoat army.

The Scottish army at Culloden had just 5,000 men but that included feeble old men and boys behind the front-line warriors. The British had almost 9,000. The Scots liked to make sudden attacks from the hills. They were not so good in an open battle like Culloden moorland. They decided to try an attack on the Redcoats before dawn. They got lost in the dark and failed. This open ground was good for cannon.

The Redcoat cannon punched great gaps in the lines of Highlanders and drove Bonnie Prince Charlie off the battlefield. When the Highlanders charged forward they were brilliantly brave … and hopelessly lost. It was a massacre, and it lasted just three-quarters of an hour.

DID YOU KNOW?

Culloden was the last battle to be fought on British soil. It was one of the most

brutal. The Duke of Cumberland gave orders that there should be no prisoners taken. The wounded who were left on the battlefield were murdered. There are even stories of Highland prisoners being burned alive.

The Bonnie Prince met a brave Highland lassie, Flora Macdonald. She risked her young life to take him across to a safe hiding place on the Isle of Skye. He dressed up in petticoats as her maidservant, Betty Burke, and as they crossed the sea, he sang Flora to sleep.

As the Redcoat net closed in, Charlie dressed in a kilt and an old shirt. He slipped through the net by crossing the heather-covered hills barefoot, through sleet and rain. When news came of a French ship off the coast he hopped onto it and went back home. He never returned to Scotland.

The Jacobite traitor wasn't very bonnie but he looked a complete Charlie when his tartan army was crushed at the Battle of Culloden.

VILE VICTORIANS

AKBAR KHAN
(1816–1847)

In 1842 Britain was at war with Russia. Queen Victoria's armies – led by the ancient General William Elphinstone – went to Afghanistan just to stop the Russians invading it. Nobody asked the Afghan people, who attacked. The British invaders were running out of food and bullets. Elphinstone decided to leave and get to the safety of India.

The journey of his 16,000 Brits led through the fearsome Khyber Pass. The Brits had to climb twice the height of Britain's highest mountain, carrying food and children. It was January and the snow was over a foot deep. People were dying of the cold before they even reached that dreadful pass. Of course the Afghans knew that. But never mind, the Afghan leader, Akbar Khan, reassured the British that they would not be attacked on their journey. The Afghan tribes simply waited for them.

Khan had betrayed them. As the Brits retreated, Akbar Khan's men attacked … horribly. The British reported that only one person out of 16,000 lived to get back safely.

General William Elphinstone died early in the retreat, before the massacre in the pass. His body was carried in a coffin down the mountain. But he wasn't allowed to rest in peace. The coffin carriers were attacked, the coffin torn open and Elphinstone's body pelted with stones.

The Afghans fought fiercely and after shooting an enemy down, they moved in to carve up the body … even if the enemy was still alive. The women followed the Afghan men to strip the bodies of anything valuable.

If the Afghan warriors missed your wounded, living body then their women would do the carving for them. Some Brits believed it was better to shoot themselves rather than be taken alive in

Afghanistan. A poem by Rudyard Kipling put it charmingly…

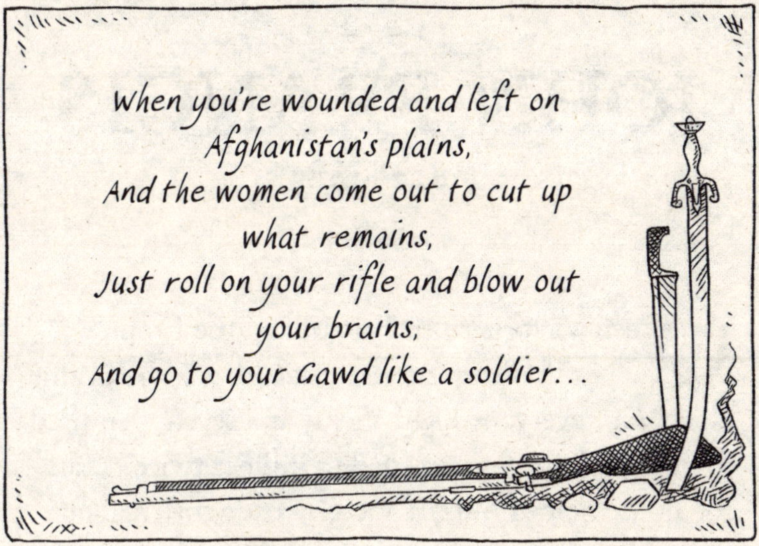

JOHN FRANCIS

(1822–1885)

Queen Victoria ruled Britain and the Empire longer than anyone else until Elizabeth II came along. Not everyone liked Vicky, and seven men tried to kill her. John Francis tried to kill her twice … and the police helped him. If Victoria had written about him in her diary it may have looked like this…

Albert and I were riding home after a church service. Albert said an evil-looking rascal pointed a gun at us. He said the pistol sparked but didn't fire and the man ran off. My dear husband reported it to Mr Peel who invented our noble police force. Peel said we had to catch him. So, he had a wonderful idea: we should ride out the next day, in the same place, and give the gunman another chance.

Albert was not in the least afraid and said it was a splendid idea.

Peel

Mr Peel had detectives in the crowd and, sure enough, a young carpenter called John Francis stepped forward and aimed his pistol. The detectives grabbed him. Imagine that? I was a real live target to catch an assassin.

Francis

The judge found him guilty and said, 'It now only remains for me to pass upon you the sentence of the law, which is that you, John Francis, be taken from hence to the place from whence you came, that you be drawn from thence on a hurdle to the place of execution and that you be hanged by the neck until you be dead; that your head be afterwards severed from your body, and that your body be divided into four quarters, to be used in such manner as to Her Majesty shall see fit. And the Lord have mercy on your soul.'

Justice

Hanged, beheaded, and cut into quarters? That sounded good to me. But my ministers told me told me to spare the traitor's life. It would make me popular, they said. Francis was transported to Australia. But I was very angry. I wanted him dead so no one tries that again.

Not justice

DID YOU KNOW?

People DID try again. The oddest one was in 1850 when Robert Pate came across Victoria in Piccadilly in London. He beat her with his metal-tipped stick and gave her a scar. Pate wasn't sure why he had done it. Like John Francis he was sent to Australia where he calmed down, and eventually came back to England with a wife and a large fortune.

FRIGHTFUL FIRST WORLD WAR

ROGER CASEMENT

(1864–1916)

Roger Casement was born in Dublin at a time when Ireland was ruled by the British. He worked for the British in Africa and came back with terrible tales of what was happening. King Leopold of Belgium was an evil ruler over millions of Africans.

Leopold wanted ivory and rubber from Africa and was a ruthless ruler. He told the workers they had to produce huge amounts and, if they failed, they were punished by…

- Cutting off the hands of men, women and children.

- Destroying whole villages and the people living there.

- Taking women and children hostage so the men had to work to set their families free.

Some historians say ten million African people died. Roger Casement was one of the first to report this cruelty and try to put a stop to it. The king made him 'Sir' Roger in 1911.

But Roger really wanted to see Ireland set free of the British rulers. In 1913 he helped to create the Irish Volunteers to give guns to Irish rebels. When Britain went to war with Germany the following year, Casement went to Germany to see how they could help the Irish fight against Britain.

When he returned to Ireland the British Army arrested him. While British soldiers were fighting and dying in the trenches in France, the Irish rebels were giving Germany a chance to attack Britain from Ireland as well. Treason. Casement was hanged as a traitor in London in 1916. Roger Casement did a lot of good work but to the British he was a traitor.

DID YOU KNOW?

Roger Casement is a hero in Ireland. Southern Ireland became free – just as Casement wanted – in 1922. In 1965 his body was dug up and sent to Ireland to be buried in the land he died for.

MATA HARI

(1876–1917)

Mata Hari was a Dutch woman who was a very popular dancer in the early 1900s. A lot of men loved to watch her dance and many of them were in the armies that were fighting against Germany.

These top French and British soldiers liked to take Mata Hari out for the evening. While they were together it is said they told her all about what they were doing. These simple-minded soldiers were traitors – they should not have been telling anyone their secrets. But they were not blamed.

Mata Hari was also loved by German officers. 'Ah,' she thought, 'I can get German secrets from them and help the French to win the war.' So, she went to the French secret service and offered to work for them.

'We don't trust you,' they said. 'You have taken money from the German officers. What was that for? Spying?'

'No,' she said. 'The German army ruined a lot of my things when they marched through my town. They were just paying me back.'

'But you told and sold them secrets?'

'Yes, but only useless old stuff that was no use to their war plans.'

'Ah,' they said (in French), 'then you are a spy. We sentence you to death.'

In 1917 Mata Hari was killed by a firing squad. Twelve years after the war the Germans said she had NOT spied for them. She died for nothing.

DID YOU KNOW?

Mata Hari was the name she used as a dancer. Her real name was Margaretha Zelle. In the 1890s she went to college. In college she learned to be what?

a) A dancer
b) A spy
c) A teacher

Answer: c) Mata Hari trained to be a teacher. Could your teacher train to be a dancer?

TERRIBLE TWENTIETH CENTURY

KIM PHILBY

(1912–1988)

Some people reach the age of 18 and stay at school. They call these schools 'universities'. There is a university in Cambridge, UK, and in the 1930s it was the home of a nest of spies. There were dozens of spies who were working for Russia. Imagine having that many spies in your school?

The worst of them was a man called Harold Philby. (But everybody called him 'Kim'.)

Kim got a great job working in the British Intelligence – which meant he was supposed to spy for Britain. But he was a traitor. His job meant he knew many secrets when Britain went into the Second World War against Germany in 1939. And what did he do? He blabbed those secrets to his Russian friends.

At the end of the war, he got a medal – the Order of the British Empire (or OBE) for his British spy work. For 30 years nobody guessed he was a traitor.

At last, in 1963, he was caught. He told his British bosses what he knew then ran off to Russia to live with his friends. He was such a hero in Russia that they put his face on a stamp. In Britain a stamp on his face would have been more likely. A stamp with a boot.

Harold 'Kim' Philby was one of the worst traitors Britain has ever seen.

DID YOU KNOW?

In the Cambridge spies there were five really bad ones. One of them, Anthony Blunt, was an expert on art. He got a job working for Queen Elizabeth II. The queen made him 'Sir Anthony' before she found out he was a spy.

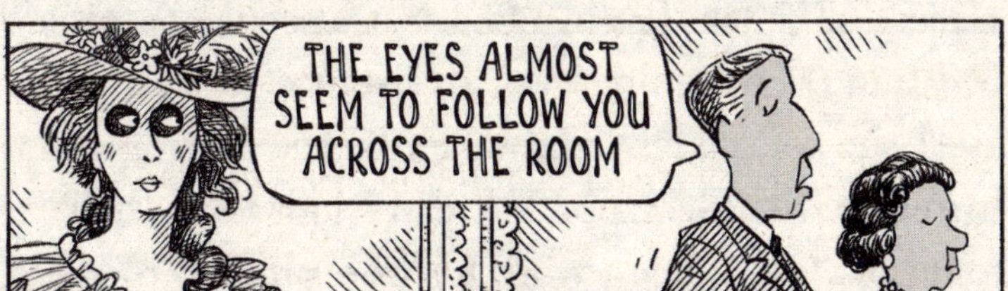

MATHILDE CARRE

(1908–2007)

In the Second World War Germany invaded France and took over. A lot of French people wanted to resist the German armies, so they became known as the 'Resistance'. The resistance wasn't an army but could make a lot of trouble for the German invaders – they'd blow up railway lines, knock down telephone cables, spy on German army secrets, and maybe tell the British the best place to drop bombs.

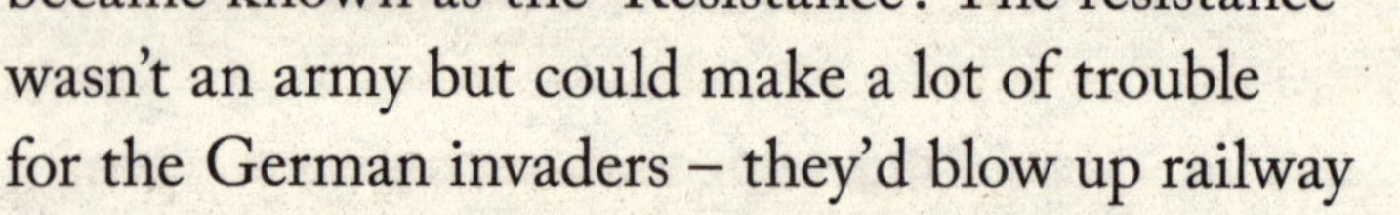

Mathilde Carre joined the Resistance. But in 1941 she was caught and taken by the fearsome torturers, the Gestapo. 'We can shoot you,' they told her. 'Or you can work for us – pretend to spy for Britain but tell us everything they are doing.'

Mathilde agreed and became a spy for the Germans and told them the names and addresses of everyone in her part of the Resistance. She even went with the Germans to arrest her French Resistance friends.

When a Resistance worker found out she was a traitor, she agreed to stop working for Germany and flee to Britain on a fast boat. Mathilde was put on trial in 1949 after the war had ended. She was told she would be executed. In fact, she was sent to prison and let out five years later. Maybe the French believed she was on their side after all.

But she gave the names and addresses to the Gestapo and SIXTY were arrested. Many were tortured and executed.

DID YOU KNOW?

Secret agents were given nicknames. Mathilde Carré was known as 'La Chatte' ('The Cat'). Like a cat she seemed to have nine lives. She died in Paris aged 98.

BLITZED BRITS

DOROTHY O'GRADY

(1897–1985)

Many traitors in Britain have been sentenced to death. But they were all men … except one. She was a woman called Dorothy O'Grady who ran a boarding house – a sort of small hotel.

O'Grady was born in London in 1897. When she was 20, she was caught forging bank notes. Three years later in 1920 she went to jail for theft. She was not an honest young woman.

In 1926 she married a London fireman called Vincent O'Grady, who was nearly 20 years older than her and ready to retire. When he left the fire service they moved to Sandown, on the Isle of Wight where they opened their boarding house. Then in 1939 the Second World War broke out and Vincent was called back for duty with the London Fire Service. When the Blitz came he'd be needed.

Back in Sandown the people were more worried about foreign spies than bombs. The beaches were closed off to stop the enemy forces landing and you couldn't walk along them. No paddling.

But Dorothy ignored the law. She took her dog Bob for walks along Culver Cliff. That was a lookout post for spotting enemy aircraft. One night Dorothy was caught flashing a light out to sea and cutting telephone wires.

When the army looked inside the lapel of her coat they found a Nazi badge – the swastika.

Her home was searched and they found maps of army defences around the Isle of Wight. Yet she wasn't arrested at once. She went on the run for three weeks.

Finally Dorothy was arrested in Yarmouth on the Isle of Wight, not far from where she lived.

O'Grady was charged with treason and sentenced to death … but she wasn't executed. She was just locked up and released in 1950.

She gave an interview to a newspaper and said…

Nobody was laughing.

DID YOU KNOW?

Some reports said O'Grady was the sort of person who enjoys pain. She really WANTED to be shot by a firing squad.

HELEN DUNCAN

(1897–1956)

Another British woman who became a traitor to spy for Germany in the Second World War was Helen Duncan.

Helen said she could talk to spirits of the dead. She had seances where she said the spirits of the dead rose up and spoke to her. People paid her money to speak to their dead friends or family. But in 1933 she was taken to court. She was a fake and she was cheating people out of their money. She was fined and moved to Portsmouth – the home of the British fleet of warships fighting Germany.

In 1941 she said she had spoken to a sailor who had been killed when his ship had been sunk. She said the ship was HMS *Barham* … and she was right about the name of the ship. It had been sunk even though the government was keeping it secret.

It was the sort of secret the enemy would like to know.

Was she a traitor? The police couldn't prove it. Still, they wanted her out of the way so she couldn't leak any more secrets. Instead of treason they charged her with a law that had been used 200 years before: the Witchcraft Act of 1735. In March 1944 she was given nine months in prison.

It could have been worse. Back in the 18th century they could have burned her at the stake.

DID YOU KNOW?

Helen Duncan let people SEE their dead friends. In the dark room they saw white stuff coming out of Duncan's mouth and it looked like a ghostly figure. In the daylight the white stuff turned out to be a roll of material like a bandage.

Helen Duncan was a fake – but we still don't know how she found out about HMS *Barham* sinking when it was a secret.

WOEFUL SECOND WORLD WAR

JOHN AMERY

(1912–1945)

Britain went to war with Germany in 1939. Men and women from Britain and its Empire signed up to join the fight. But a tiny number signed up to fight for Germany. They were known as the British Free Corps (BFC). Traitors.

In 1942 John Amery went across to Germany and told Hitler's army, 'I know you are fighting against Russia. I hate Russia and want to help you. Let me put together a team of British and Empire men who will fight for you.' Adolf Hitler thought it was a great idea. On his birthday, 20 April, the BFC got their own special uniforms. Very smart.

Many British soldiers had been captured and were held in prisoner-of-war camps. Avery went to talk to them and invited them to join his army. They were promised a good life and freedom from the camps. Over the next couple of years around 50 men joined Amery's BFC. Not many then.

Amery left Germany to fight for another enemy of Britain, Italy. He was captured and handed back to the British. He said, 'Yes, I joined the Germans, but I NEVER fought against Britain.' It made no difference. His trial lasted eight minutes, he was found guilty, and he was hanged for treason. The other BFC members were sent to prison.

DID YOU KNOW?

Amery's father Leo AND his brother Julian were both members of parliament.

WILLIAM JOYCE LORD HAW-HAW

(1906–1946)

Not every traitor in the Second World War picked up a gun to fight against Britain. William Joyce picked up a microphone. He went across to Germany and sent radio messages to the people in Britain. He wanted them to give up the war. He began his broadcast, 'Germany calling, Germany calling.' His voice was so posh it sounded like 'Jairmany colling, Jairmany colling'. The ordinary people of Britain called him 'Lord Haw-Haw'.

He said things like…

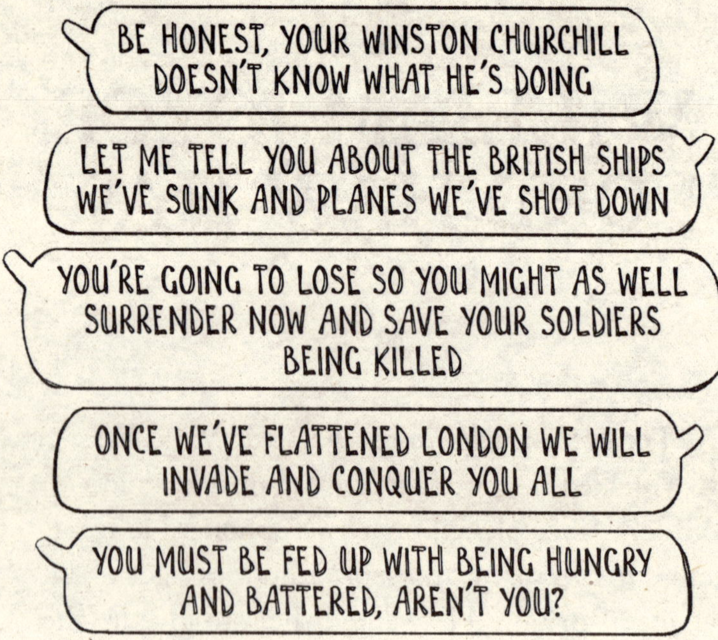

Just like Amery and the British Free Corps traitors, Joyce said the real enemy was Russia and he joined the Germans to fight them.

When Germany started to lose the war and the Allies invaded Germany, Joyce knew he was in trouble. The traitor went into hiding. Two British soldiers knocked on his door as they were out looking for firewood. They arrested him. How did they know he was Lord Haw-Haw? From his voice, of course. Joyce was shot in the leg and taken back to Britain. He was hanged for treason.

He was the last person to be executed for treason in the United Kingdom.

EPILOGUE

Traitors have been around for thousands of years. From Mithridates who lied to get power in 116 BC to Helen Duncan who lied for money in 1941. Some of their betrayals cost their friends and countrymen thousands of lives. Some, like Francis Tresham and the Gunpowder Plot, SAVED hundreds of lives.

There will probably be traitors around for another few thousand years. YOU could be a traitor. Just remember a lot of the traitors ended up very unhappy or very dead in horrible ways.

What would turn YOU into a traitor?

INDEX

Where will you find bums (pains in the), grave-robbers and a pickled Parliamentarian in an index? In a *Horrible Histories* book, of course!

TERRY DEARY

Terry Deary was born at a very early age, so long ago he can't remember. But his mother, who was there at the time, says he was born in Sunderland, northeast England, in 1946 – so it's not true that he writes all Horrible Histories from memory. At school he was a horrible child only interested in playing football and giving teachers a hard time. His history lessons were so boring and so badly taught, that he learned to loathe the subject. Horrible Histories is his revenge.

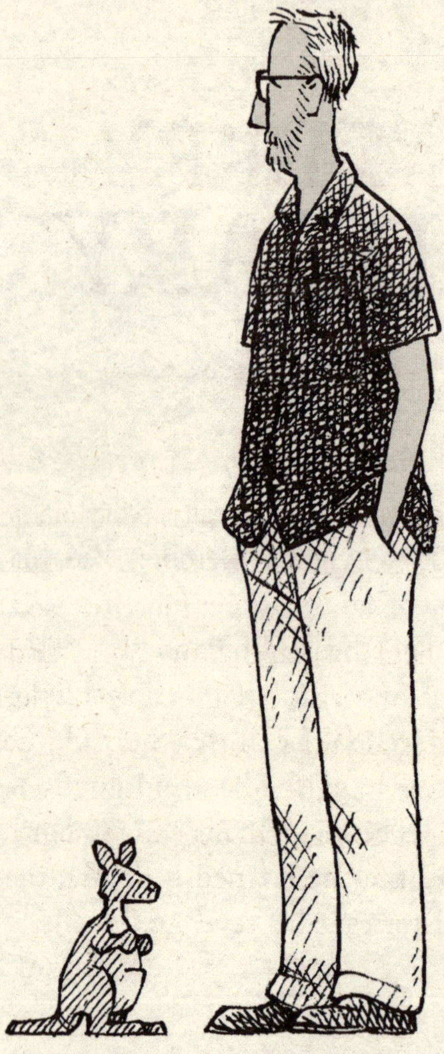

MARTIN BROWN

Martin Brown was born in Melbourne, on the proper side of the world. Ever since he can remember he's been drawing. His dad used to bring back huge sheets of paper from work and Martin would fill them with doodles and little figures. Then, quite suddenly, with food and water, he grew up, moved to the UK and found work doing what he's always wanted to do: drawing doodles and little figures.